**For my sister Kate,
who taught me that standing
out can be a superpower.**

NORTHERN LIGHTS

Winnie Harlow

SUPERMODEL • ENTREPRENEUR • ACTIVIST

AMY LAND

PLUMLEAF PRESS

Note

The "Spotlight" feature is informational text that the author has written to add contextual depth to the topics being presented in the biography. Bolded words are defined in the glossary on page 56.

CONTENTS

CHAPTER 1
A True Game Changer

Imagine a young girl in Toronto playing the life-simulation video game *The Sims*. In the game, she builds a beautiful home for her character and dreams of one day living there. There was one problem, though ...

This girl was Winnie Harlow. She would grow up to become a famous Canadian supermodel. When she played *The Sims*, she couldn't make her character look like herself. That's because Winnie has a condition called vitiligo *(vit-uh-LIE-go)*, which makes some patches of skin lose their colour.

Many years later, in February 2024, Winnie changed the game. She teamed up with *The Sims 4* to add vitiligo skin features. Now, players can create characters with vitiligo — and even play as Winnie herself!

In the game, you can also visit Winnie's house, which looks just like her real mansion in Los Angeles. It even has a glam room filled with her framed magazine covers.

"I really worked for the little Winnie who'd never seen herself **represented**," she said. "If I was able to talk to my younger self, I think I would just cry. I would tell her to never give up, and that even on your lowest days, remember that there's always a brighter future. And I would have loved to be able to show her *this* [the game's vitiligo features] as that brighter future."

Spotlight: The Science of Vitiligo

Have you ever wondered what gives your skin its colour?

Your skin gets its colour from special cells called melanocytes. These make melanin, a pigment that gives skin, hair, and eyes their colour. Melanin also helps protect your skin from the sun.

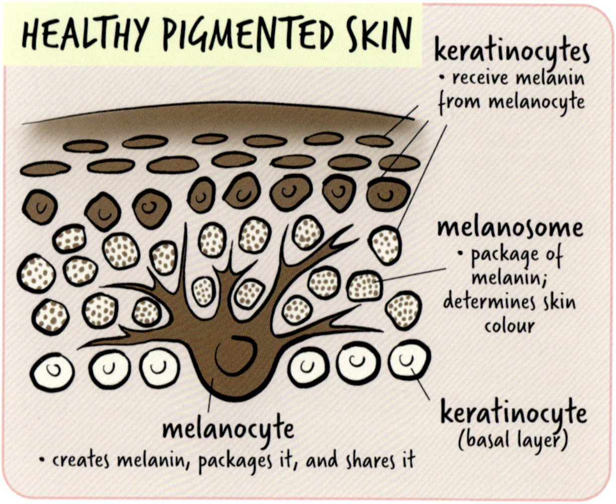

People of all skin colours have about the same number of melanocytes. What makes skin darker or lighter is how much melanin those cells produce. People with darker skin make more melanin. People with lighter skin make less.

VITILIGO: UNDER THE SURFACE

Vitiligo happens when the body's immune system (white blood cells) attacks the melanocytes by mistake. When melanocytes are damaged, the skin in certain areas stops making melanin. This causes white patches to appear.

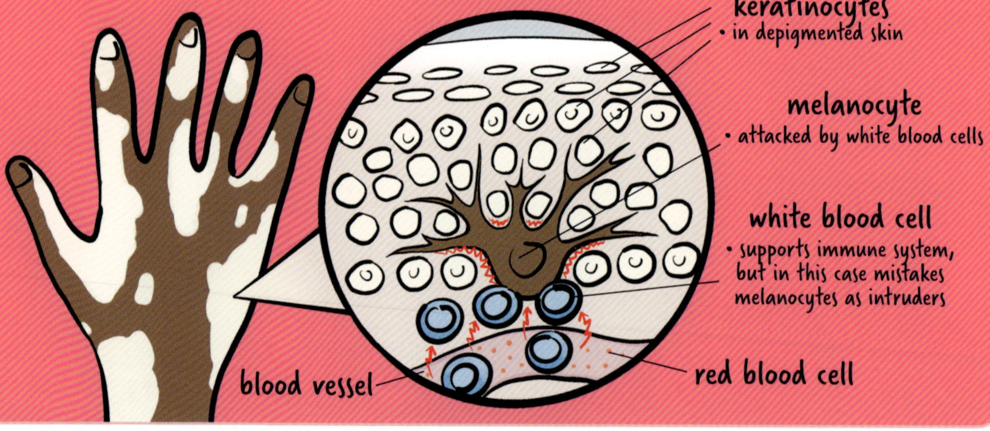

Quick Facts About Vitiligo

1. Vitiligo is not contagious — you can't catch it from someone.
2. About 1 out of every 100 people in the world has vitiligo.
3. It can affect people of all skin colours, but it's often more noticeable on darker skin.
4. Vitiligo can start at any age, but it often begins before age 30.
5. Vitiligo doesn't hurt, but looking different can sometimes make people feel sad, anxious, or left out.
6. Some people choose to cover their patches, but many — like Winnie Harlow — choose to show them proudly.

OTHER FAMOUS PEOPLE WITH VITILIGO

Michael Jackson
(pop star)

Jon Hamm
(actor)

CHAPTER 2
Growing Up Different

When Winnie Harlow was little, she was bullied so much that she would sometimes sit by the window and stare up at the stars, wishing her skin condition would disappear. As a little girl growing up in the Toronto suburbs, the daughter of Jamaican Canadian parents, she felt like she didn't fit in. Her mother raised her, and she would go and visit her father in Jamaica twice a year at Christmastime and for the summer.

When she was four years old, she developed vitiligo, which caused patches of her skin to lose their colour. At first, she didn't understand why people stared. But as she got older, the stares turned into whispers. Then the whispers turned into teasing.

FLASH-FACT

Winnie Harlow's birth name is Chantelle Brown-Young. She chose "Winnie" after Winnie-the-Pooh and "Harlow" after a tough-minded 1930s Hollywood actress named Jean Harlow.

Changing schools didn't help, either. It's hard enough being the new kid, let alone the new kid with a visible skin condition. At one school, Winnie finally made two new friends. For a while, everything seemed better. She and her friends laughed and played at recess, and shared snacks at lunch. Then, after a few weeks, the girls suddenly stopped talking to her.

Winnie worked up the courage to ask her friends why they were not talking to her. They told her, "Our parents said we might catch your skin condition."

Winnie was only in grade two.

That moment hurt a lot. Over time, the pain of being stared at and rejected started to build. Students would often call her "zebra" or "cow." Then, when she was 13, she experienced the unthinkable at a school assembly. As she walked into the auditorium, one student started yelling "Moo! MOOOOOooo!" Then, slowly, more and more students joined in.

Eventually, Winnie began pushing people away before they could hurt her. She even admitted that she decided to become a bully for a little while. It was her way to protect herself from more heartbreak.

Winnie's family tried to help her feel confident. For family photos, her mom would gently apply makeup to even out her skin tone. Her mother wanted to help her feel beautiful, but it didn't always work.

"I obviously didn't feel comfortable," Winnie would later explain. Her mom's makeup paste was heavy and too dark. It didn't match Winnie's skin, and it just felt wrong.

Winnie's white patches didn't have melanin, which meant they couldn't protect her from the sun. She hated having to wear long sleeves and stockings under her clothes. She also hated feeling like she had to cover up. Slowly, though, things started to change.

Books became a place where Winnie could escape. She was a bookworm with a big imagination, but school still felt like a struggle. Like many kids who feel different, Winnie worked hard to fit in — even if it meant ignoring who she really was. She cared more about sitting with the "cool kids" than paying attention in class. Eventually, her vice-principal recommended an alternative school. At this school, Winnie could go there just for her classes and then go home. That change helped her refocus on her learning and not worry so much about trying to fit in.

Winnie began to care less about what other people thought and more about how she felt. When people stared, she didn't hide. When they judged her, she ignored them.

FLASH-FACT

When Winnie was in grade 5, she won a reading competition because she had read the most books in the entire school.

Even though Winnie never dreamed of being a model, people around her started to notice something special. Friends asked her to walk in small community fashion shows or pose for local clothing brands. Some even said they could picture her on the cover of the fashion magazine *Vogue*. At first, Winnie didn't believe it because she didn't see anyone who looked like her in any magazines.

One day, she decided to start posting photos of herself on Instagram. The response was good. People saw her beauty and her bravery. Slowly, Winnie began to see it too. She was ready to start showing the world exactly who she was.

CHAPTER 3
Unstoppable

When Winnie Harlow was 16, she took the bus to Toronto's Yorkdale Mall to apply for a job at Sephora. She felt it would be the perfect fit because she loved everything to do with makeup and skincare. Not to mention, she wanted the chance to earn some money and then spend it on store products while getting an employee discount. As perfect as it was, the store said no. That day, she got an early lesson in rejection, but it wouldn't be her last.

At the time, Winnie was doing some small modelling gigs for friends. A few people told her that she had real talent. So, she and her mom visited some modelling agencies in downtown Toronto. At one agency, an executive looked at her and said something Winnie would never forget.

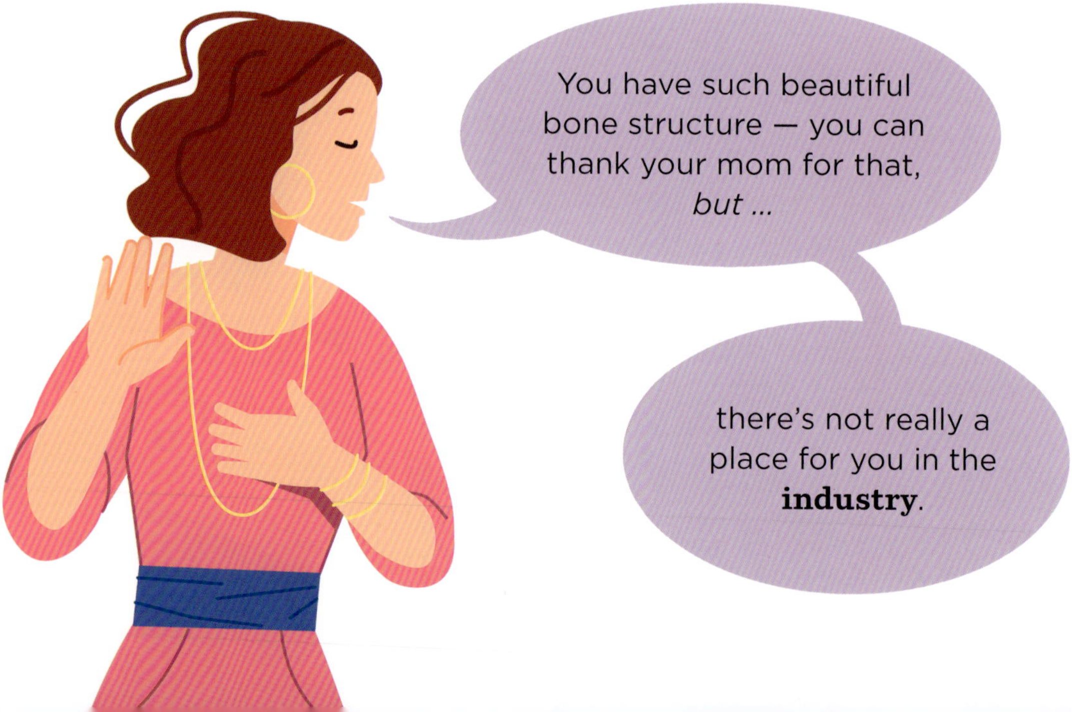

> ***I never took any 'no's' as 'No.' I took it as 'maybe later' or 'not right now.'***

The executive didn't stop there. Just to make things worse, this person said that if Winnie wanted to be "anywhere near" the fashion world, she should try being a makeup artist — behind the camera.

Back in the early 2010s, most models in magazines and on TV looked the same. Models with vitiligo were not represented in the mainstream fashion world at all. Many models were white and thin with similar features. There wasn't much room for someone who looked like Winnie. That didn't mean that she was going to give up, though.

"I never took any 'no's' as 'No,' she later said about the experience. "I took it as 'maybe later' or 'not right now.'"

Strength Runs in the Family

Where does Winnie get her determination? She says it comes from her family, especially her grandmother. "I'm a very strong, fiery Caribbean woman," Winnie explained. A lot of that comes from her grandmother. "I'm very proud that I've had such a strong woman to look up to, to give me that courage."

When Winnie was a little girl, another child pointed at her and asked, "What's that on your skin?"

When Winnie responded, she sounded exactly like her grandmother when she sassily said to the girl, "Child, it's none of your business."

Lights, Camera, and Another No

It's clear that Winnie was not a shy teenager. Modelling wasn't her only dream. She also wanted to be on TV. At 17, she heard about a contest from the music video network MTV Canada. They were looking for a new VJ (video jockey) to host shows and interview celebrities.

Winnie stood in a long line of hopefuls. Again, she heard the word NO.

The MTV team told her she didn't have enough experience. They suggested she study journalism. This stung, but Winnie was not derailed. She kept going. Winnie was on a mission.

Eyes on the Prize

Shannon Boodram, a journalist and educator, has been Winnie's friend since the early days. Here she talks about why she admires Winnie:

"Winnie is not a self-pitier. There are so many moments when I'll message her saying, 'Can you believe this?' or 'Can you believe that?' and she responds with such calm and grounded clarity.

> ***I'm a train, and I know where I'm going. If people don't want to get on now, they can catch up at future stops.***

One example I can think of comes from her early days pursuing modelling representation. Agency after agency turned her away and even told her this probably wasn't the right lane for her. I was furious. I wanted to defend her, to reframe it in a way I thought would be encouraging. But she stopped me and said, 'It doesn't matter. I'm a train, and I know where I'm going. If people don't want to get on now, they can catch up at future stops.'

And that's exactly who she has continued to be. A train that prioritizes the destiny she sees for herself over the personal slights that would derail many of us along the way."

The Message That Changed Everything

Around this time, *America's Next Top Model (ANTM)* was looking for contestants for a new season. Winnie had a bold idea. She asked her Instagram followers to tag the show's host, Tyra Banks, in any photos of Winnie. She even got some help from her little sister, who created a Facebook page to show off Winnie's modelling.

Winnie's plan worked. One day, Winnie checked her inbox and saw a message from an *ANTM* producer. They asked if she wanted to audition for the show. At first, Winnie thought it was fake, but it wasn't. Winnie joined Season 21 of *America's Next Top Model*, making history as the show's first contestant with vitiligo.

"After Tyra gave me that opportunity, it was my time."

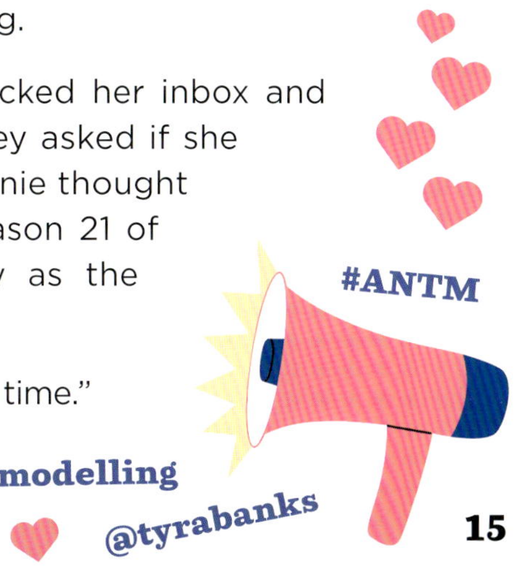

Spotlight: How To Bounce Back From Disappointment

Winnie Harlow faced many tough moments when life didn't go her way, but she didn't let the hard times stop her from shining. Everyone is going to experience tough times and setbacks. When you feel down or disappointed about something, remember: those feelings are normal, and, just like Winnie, you can get through them and you'll be stronger. Try these steps below when things feel tough.

- **Stop and take a deep breath.**
  Try to name what you're feeling (angry, sad, hurt, disappointed, embarrassed, and so on). It's okay to feel upset. Feelings are important.

- **Be kind to yourself.**
  Remember that one problem doesn't make you who you are. Sometimes it just means that things need more time or you need to try something else.

- **Talk it out.**
  Find someone who cares about you (friend, parent, caregiver, teacher, and so on), and tell them how you're feeling. Sometimes just saying the problem out loud makes you feel a lot better.

- **Think of Winnie.**
  Your uniqueness is your power. What makes you special and strong? Celebrate it instead of trying to hide it. Winnie helped a lot of people with differences feel seen because she didn't give up.

Create Your Own Power Phrase!

Think of a short, strong phrase that helps you feel brave and ready to keep going. Here are some examples to get you started.

I am brave.

I can figure this out.

Mistakes help me grow.

I've got this.

I'm unstoppable.

I shine my own way.

CHAPTER 4
Winnie's Next Challenge

What happened to Winnie next was the stuff that dreams are made of — sort of. Before she could compete on *America's Next Top Model*, she had to audition for the show's famous host, Tyra Banks. When it came to modelling, Tyra was an expert because she was a supermodel.

At the audition, 19-year-old Winnie, who still went by her real name Chantelle, walked onto the stage alone. The cameras were rolling.

In front of her sat Tyra and two other judges.

Tyra told the others that she had found Winnie on social media. Then she didn't waste any time before bringing up Winnie's skin condition.

"I've actually never seen vitiligo that way," Tyra said. "It's like **symmetrical** fantastic-ness."

Winnie, who was wearing a tank top and skirt, smiled proudly and lifted her arms to show her unique markings. She wasn't hiding who she was. She was celebrating it.

> ***"It's like symmetrical fantastic-ness."***

Then Tyra asked Winnie a serious question: Had she been bullied?

Winnie nodded and told the judges about the pain of being teased and misunderstood. Then she shared something surprising. "People have actually asked me if my mom is white and my dad is Black, and I wasn't mixed properly in the belly."

Tyra looked shocked. "And how old was that person?" she asked.

"My age," Winnie said.

Tyra then dished out some real talk: "I'm going to say something harsh," she warned. "If you have something like vitiligo ... people tend to soft tread. If you get into this competition, I will not soft tread. I will be just as harsh on you as everyone else."

The big word in Tyra's speech was only two letters long:

Stepping Into the Spotlight

Tyra's "if" quickly turned into a "yes." In 2014, Winnie had made it onto Cycle 21 of *America's Next Top Model*, but the real test was only just beginning.

One part of the show took the contestants all the way to South Korea. During a photoshoot there, the photographer, Yu Tsai, called Winnie his "little panda bear." It was one thing to get teased by classmates, but to be called names by a professional on national television? Ouch. Still, Winnie stayed calm. She acted like a grown-up.

After the shoot, she walked up to Yu and asked him not to call her that again. He got defensive. He said he was just trying to help.

Winnie didn't yell. She didn't back down, either. She said that she knew he wasn't trying to be mean with the nickname.

She then explained, "I don't want kids out there to see you, someone so high up in the industry, being able to call me 'panda' and then see somebody else with a skin condition and be like, 'Hey, Yu Tsai could call [Winnie] panda, I can call this person a cow.'"

Later in the episode, Yu made a harsh prediction. He said that Winnie is "not going to make it in the modelling industry if she keeps this attitude that she has."

He couldn't have been more wrong.

FLASH-FACT

Out of the 14 contestants on Cycle 21 of *America's Next Top Model*, Winnie was the only Canadian.

Fan Favourite

As dramatic as Winnie's time on *America's Next Top Model* was, it didn't last too long. She stayed in the model house for just two episodes before she was cut from the show for having the lowest score that week. This didn't mean it was time for her to go home, though.

This season of *ANTM* had something new — *The Comeback Series*. It meant that fans could vote online for their favourite contestants. This would give eliminated models a chance to return to the show if they got enough votes.

After Winnie was cut, she kept doing photoshoots for the show behind the scenes. These photos were shared online, and fans could keep voting for her. The fans loved Winnie! Her bold look and confidence made her stand out. People were talking about her and sharing her photos on social media. She ended up with the highest score of all the eliminated contestants and got to return to the show in Episode 9.

This moment showed that Winnie's voice and presence were powerful.

Time for Bigger Things

Even with all of the attention she got from being on *America's Next Top Model*, Winnie didn't feel like the show had helped her in the way she hoped. She even said that no agency would sign her because they had negative opinions about reality TV.

In Winnie's opinion, her real big break didn't come from the show. In fact, she said that after she came off *America's Next Top Model*, she was considering quitting modelling and going back to school for journalism. Before that could happen, though, someone else found her on Instagram — someone who saw her as a serious model.

That someone was Nick Knight, a famous fashion photographer. He had worked with major magazines, fashion designers, and supermodels. Nick invited Winnie to do a professional photoshoot. This time, there were no judges, no voting, and no one calling her names.

Even early in her career, Winnie's confidence shone through at New York Fashion Week in 2015.

Spotlight: How To Spot a Publicity Stunt

Is It Real ... or Just for Show?

Sometimes, people, brands, politicians, or shows do things to get attention, especially on TV or social media. These moments are called publicity stunts. They can be funny, emotional, or shocking, but the real goal is to make headlines, sell something, or go viral. It's like free advertising.

Here are a few ways to tell if something might be a publicity stunt. Keep them in mind the next time you're online.

Is someone suddenly everywhere?

If a person or story pops up all over the Internet for saying or doing something strange, ask: Would this still matter if cameras weren't around?

Is it focused on shock, not meaning?

If the focus is on how surprising, weird, or offensive it is (and not why it matters), it might be more about getting clicks than telling the truth.

Does it make you forget the bigger picture?

Sometimes stunts are used to take everyone's attention away from a bad story or important issue, and pay attention to the staged story instead. Try to look at the whole story and not just the loudest part.

Does it feel too dramatic or perfectly timed?

If something wild happens right before a big product launch or show episode, it might be staged to grab your attention.

Ask Yourself:

Who benefits from this moment being shared and how?

CHAPTER 5
The New Face of Fashion

Winnie's time on *America's Next Top Model* did not make her want to choose modelling as a career. In fact, some experiences on the show made her question it altogether. On one episode, a judge looked at her and said, "Wow! You're like an X-Man! But can you model?" Ugh.

The world would soon find out the answer to that question: A huge, confident

"*YES!*"

Winnie Harlow could model, and she was just getting started.

London Calling

While most *Top Model* contestants faded into the background after the show ended, Winnie's journey was just heating up. Even though she was unsure about her next steps, she took a leap of faith. She decided to accept the offer from top British fashion photographer Nick Knight to do a photoshoot.

Before long, Winnie was on a plane to London.

"He gave me my first **campaign**," she said. "That was the beginning of it." She even calls Knight her "fashion godfather."

"I wouldn't have a career without him," Winnie explained. "Nick Knight was my first big gig as a 'real' model ... I was 19, and that shoot was a magical experience."

The photos were stunning. They got attention from the fashion world, and big brands started calling. This time, Winnie wasn't just standing out. She was breaking through.

From that moment on, doors began to open. Winnie landed major fashion shoots and walked in international runway shows. More and more brands were realizing that models didn't all have to look the same, and audiences were loving it.

People were drawn to Winnie. Her confidence. Her style. Her story. With every new job, she was changing the definition of beauty itself.

Winnie had a mission. Soon, she wouldn't only be seen, she would be heard.

Changing Minds

Winnie's modelling career was taking off. She was travelling the world, starring in fashion shows, and appearing on magazine covers. For a lot of people, that would be enough. But not for Winnie.

She didn't just want to be in front of the camera — she wanted to help people think differently. She wanted to open their minds up about beauty.

In 2014, Winnie gave a powerful TEDxTeen talk called "How I Define Beauty." TED talks are short speeches where people share big ideas, and Winnie had something unforgettable to say.

She walked onto the stage with confidence and asked the audience a surprising question: "What do you find most beautiful ... in a person?"

She gave some examples, asking, "Is it pretty eyes? Blue eyes? Curly hair? Long nails? Big feet?"

The crowd laughed, but she had made her point. A lot of what we think is "beautiful" comes from outside voices: social media, magazines, and movies. But what if those voices are wrong?

> **"Know for yourself what beauty is rather than looking to a magazine or even me for what beauty is."**

Winnie's TED talk has now been viewed nearly 1.5 million times.

Winnie told the audience how she used to get bullied for her skin. It hurt so much that she started bullying others just to protect herself. That moment of honesty took real courage. What she said next was even more powerful.

She said she stopped trying to change who she was. She stopped trying to fit in. Instead, she built her own definition of beauty and encouraged everyone else to do the same.

She reminded the audience that they don't need to fit into anyone else's mould. "It takes one person to realize there is beauty in everything," she said.

"Know for yourself what beauty is rather than looking to a magazine or even me for what beauty is."

Winnie wasn't just changing minds — she was helping people love themselves.

Spotlight: Who's Defining Your Beauty?

Use this flowchart to figure out if you are seeing your real self or what the world is telling you to see ...

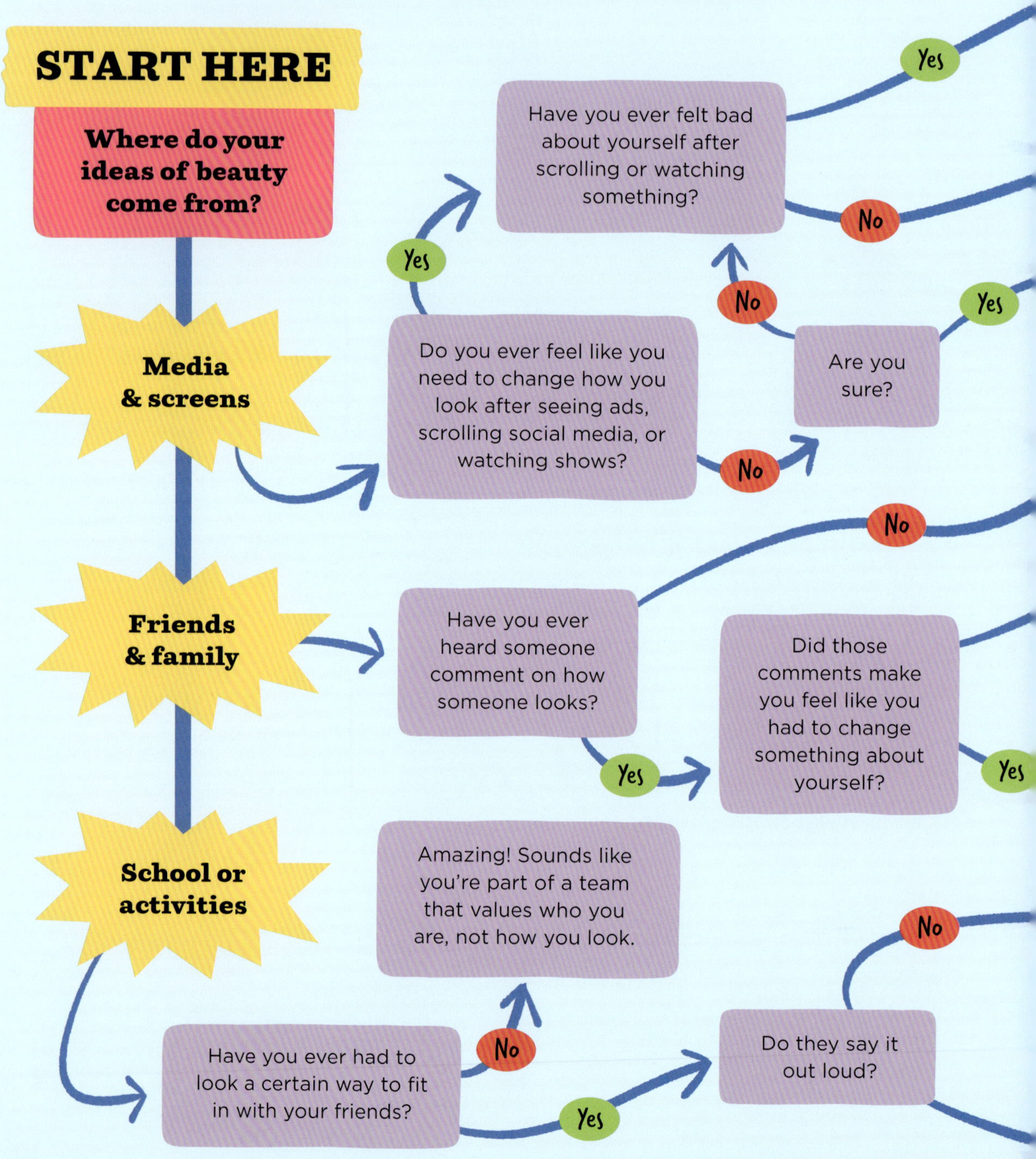

Hmm. Could editing, filters, and paid promotions be shaping how you feel?

Cool! You might already know that what's online isn't always real.

Nice! Your circle helps you feel confident. Real support = real beauty.

No

That's cool. You might be carving your own path without outside pressure.

Think about it: Do their ideas lift you up or stress you out?

That's sneaky pressure. Time to ask: Who decided those rules?

Yes

Hmm. Saying it out loud doesn't make it true.

Watch out!

You might be chasing someone else's idea of beauty. Think about who is behind the camera. What is their message?

You've got a strong inner filter!

It takes guts to scroll past the noise and listen to yourself. That's real strength. Keep it up!

Time to create your own beauty rules.

Winnie didn't change to please anyone. YOU are the boss of your self-image. Keep what feels right and let the rest go.

You set the standards.

Even if others expect certain things, you decide what matters.

Walking in the Victoria's Secret fashion show is like the Olympics of modelling. When Winnie found out she was in, she was so overwhelmed, she dropped everything and burst into tears of joy.

CHAPTER 6
Winnie Claps Back

As Winnie kept setting career goals, year after year, she kept knocking them down. She walked in the Victoria's Secret fashion show, she was a Puma brand ambassador, and she appeared in Beyoncé's visual album *Lemonade*. Her name was on everyone's lips, but there was one word that rubbed her the wrong way.

A 2018 photo caption in a London, UK, newspaper called her a "Canadian vitiligo sufferer." Winnie was not having it. She posted a photo of the newspaper on Instagram and wrote: "I'm not a 'vitiligo sufferer.' I'm not a 'vitiligo model.' I am Winnie. I am a model. And I happen to have vitiligo. Stop putting these titles on me or anyone else."

Winnie made her message crystal clear. She continued, "I AM NOT SUFFERING. If anything I'm SUCCEEDING at showing people that their differences don't make them WHO they are."

"I'm sick of every headline ending in 'vitiligo sufferer' or 'suffers from vitiligo.'" She then asked a big question: "Do you see me suffering? The only thing I'm suffering from are your headlines and the closed minds of humans who have one beauty standard locked into their minds when there are multiple standards of beauty!"

> *"I'm not a 'vitiligo sufferer.' I'm not a 'vitiligo model.' I am Winnie. I am a model. And I happen to have vitiligo."*

Spotlight: Think Before You Speak

Why Words Matter

Inclusive Language

Some words might seem small, but they can have a big impact. When we describe someone only by a condition, challenge, or background, we risk shrinking who they really are.

Take the word "sufferer." It sounds like the person is in pain or needs pity. That's why Winnie spoke up when a newspaper called her a "vitiligo sufferer." She wasn't suffering — she was succeeding.

Using respectful, **inclusive language** helps everyone feel valued. It shows that people are more than just one thing, and that no one should be judged by how they look, move, learn, or live.

Instead of ...	Try saying ...
"That's crazy."	"That's confusing."
"Hey, guys!"	"Hey, everyone!"
Old people	Older people
Policeman	Police officer
Confined to a wheelchair	Uses a wheelchair
Slow learner	Student who needs extra help

Quick Tip:

For a small change that shows big respect, use people-first language. That means saying what someone has instead of what they are. For example, instead of calling someone "a diabetic," say they are "a person with diabetes."

CHAPTER 7
Real Love, Real Talk

Winnie's life was full of big, exciting moments. There were the fashion shows, magazine covers, and global campaigns, of course, but she would soon have a big change in her personal life. It came from a place she knew well: her Instagram DMs.

In 2019, NBA basketball player Kyle Kuzma sent Winnie a message ... but she didn't see it until almost a year later!

It must have been a "glitch in the system," she later joked. Kyle didn't give up, though. The next year, he posted an Instagram story congratulating her on her Puma deal. This time she noticed (phew!) and messaged him back.

They started texting, FaceTiming, and bonding with each other from opposite sides of the United States. It was during the COVID-19 pandemic, so they had a lot of time to talk, play games like *21 Questions*, and even watch movies "together" by pressing play at the same time.

Winnie was in Brooklyn, and Kyle was in Los Angeles, but their long-distance friendship turned into something more. In June 2020, they became Instagram-official. For Valentine's Day in 2021, Winnie posted a message thanking Kyle for being her shoulder to cry on and hand to hold.

By July 2022, she was calling Kyle "the best boyfriend in the world." In August 2023, she got a small tattoo of his name behind her ear. Then, in April 2024, Winnie and Kyle celebrated their fourth anniversary.

Less than a year later, Kyle planned something unforgettable.

He chartered a plane so that they could fly to the Turks and Caicos Islands for Valentine's Day. The plane was filled with balloons, roses, and chocolate. Then Kyle read Winnie a poem he had written that ended with one big question: "Will you marry me?"

> **"*Will you marry me?*"**

In a couples quiz, when Winnie asked Kyle what three things she taught him, he said, "Gotta have patience, gotta communicate and, you have to understand where other people are coming from."

A surprised Winnie said,

"YES!"

As in love as Winnie is, she knows that a happy relationship takes more than roses and poems. In a podcast interview, Winnie explained why she and Kyle started couples **counselling** before they got engaged. She wanted them to grow strong together from the start.

"We've been talking about engagement for the past year. We started doing marriage counselling and just communicating," Winnie said. "I think it's so important to learn good communication before you even take that step."

It is clear that Winnie knows how to lead with her heart and her head. "Whatever relationship, whether it's with your parents, with your friends, there's always going to be obstacles in life," she said. But she knows that learning how to talk things through and understanding each other is what makes a relationship strong.

Spotlight: Healthy Relationship Survival Kit

Whether it's your best friend, a parent, a teacher or someone you like, good relationships don't just happen — they are built. Think of the following list as your survival kit for keeping connections strong and drama low.

Trust Is The VIP Pass

What it is: Trust

What it looks like: You can count on the other person, and they can count on you.

Winnie-style: Winnie and Kyle built trust slowly. Before meeting in person, they shared their thoughts, dreams, and fears on FaceTime during the pandemic. No pressure, just real talk.

Your Lines, Your Rules

What it is: Boundaries

What it looks like: You feel safe saying "no" when something doesn't feel right, and the other person respects it.

Winnie-style: On *America's Next Top Model*, Winnie told a photographer not to call her his "little panda bear." She drew a line and she stuck to it.

No Mind Reading Allowed

What it is: Communication

What it looks like: You listen as much as you talk, and you check in often.

Winnie-style: Before getting married, Winnie and Kyle went to counselling. She wanted to build a strong **foundation** *before* problems came up.

Kindness Is Never Out of Style

What it is: Respect

What it looks like: You treat each other kindly, even when you don't agree.

Winnie-style: Growing up, Winnie's family respected her for who she was. This helped her feel strong, even when other people didn't treat her well.

Bounce Back Together

What it is: Problem-solving

What it looks like: You work through the hard stuff as a team.

Winnie-style: With her global modelling jobs and Kyle's NBA career, their schedules don't always match. Instead of letting that pull them apart, they make plans to connect and adjust when things change.

CHAPTER 8
Boss Moves

When Winnie was a teenager, she didn't get a job with the big beauty store Sephora. Imagine, though, if someone had told her back then that one day she'd own her very own beauty brand with products sold in Sephora stores!

Winnie's story is a good example of how following your passion and solving a problem can lead to powerful business ideas. In March 2022, Winnie launched her very own skincare brand called Cay Skin. It took almost three years of testing to get her products just right.

The idea for Cay Skin came from a tough experience during a photo shoot in the Caribbean back in 2018. No one on the team wanted her to reapply sunscreen because it left a white layer on her skin that showed up in photos. As a result, Winnie got badly sunburned. Not only was it very painful, but it also changed the look of her vitiligo forever.

Winnie says that the experience left her "scarred physically and emotionally." She knew that she had to create a better sunscreen. She obsessed over every detail of her products, even using ingredients inspired by her Jamaican heritage. Eventually, she was able to create something that protects all skin tones without leaving a white cast.

> ***"Winnie's story is a good example of how following your passion and solving a problem can lead to powerful business ideas."***

Big Wins for Winnie

When Cay Skin came out, Winnie was praised for joining a very small group of women of colour who have raised more than $1 million in venture capital, aka money that helps businesses grow. In total, she raised $4.1 million to launch her brand. Today, Cay Skin is sold at Sephora stores across Canada and the United States.

Winnie is a Black female founder in the very competitive skincare industry. With Cay Skin, she's helping to make products work for all kinds of skin, including the darker skin tones that were often ignored before.

Winnie says, "I'm so proud of the work I've done to change the face of the beauty industry, both as a model and now as a Black female entrepreneur. I look forward to pushing for more change that puts Black women in the driver's seat."

Winnie's Home Sweet Home

Winnie Harlow's "firsts" list is full of amazing and surprising moments — from being the first supermodel with vitiligo to the first person with vitiligo to have a wax figure at Madame Tussauds! But did you know that she also had a pretty cool first home?

FLASH-FACT

In 2024, Winnie sold her first home for $3.6 million.

Every successful boss needs a home that matches their style, and Winnie's first house was so stylish it was featured in a design magazine.

After years of renting apartments, Winnie wanted a place with lots of sunshine and a beautiful pool. Los Angeles seemed like the perfect spot. Of course, it helped that her new boyfriend, Kyle, lived there too! By the end of 2020, Winnie bought a huge five-bedroom place. This was the house that was recreated in the video game *The Sims*, where Winnie was a character.

Winnie wanted her home to feel chill and glamorous at the same time. The designer added special touches to celebrate her modelling career. He made wallpaper from her campaign test photos, and her glam room features a whole wall of framed magazine covers featuring Winnie. She said the cover wall "turned into more of a moment of gratitude and appreciation for how far I've come."

She also filled her home with photos of models like Beverly Johnson and Grace Jones. "These amazing Black women are people who made pathways for me to walk," Winnie said. "I get to wake up every day and see those trailblazers on my wall."

CHAPTER 9
Helping Others Shine

When Winnie steps into the spotlight, she doesn't keep it all for herself — she lights up people around her. Whether it's celebrating someone's Halloween costume or speaking on a global stage alongside Michelle Obama, Winnie knows that success feels better when you share it.

Leading by Example

Imagine having a secret so big that you spend hours every morning trying to hide it. That was life for Tiffany Taylor. Her vitiligo first appeared at a pretty stressful time: She was 14 and just entering high school. Each day, she would get up early to layer on makeup and self-tanner from head to toe, determined to keep her difference hidden from the world.

"My family supported me covering the vitiligo with makeup," Tiffany explained. "It was their way of dealing, best as they knew how."

Then everything changed.

In 2017, Tiffany walked into a Halloween party dressed as Winnie Harlow. For the first time in years, her vitiligo was on full display. The reaction? People were impressed, curious, and supportive. This inspired Tiffany to post a side-by-side photo online: Tiffany in Winnie's exact outfit, nailing the same confident pose.

The post blew up with encouraging comments. Then came the biggest surprise of all ... Winnie herself shared Tiffany's photo on Instagram, instantly giving it a global spotlight.

Seeing Winnie living her best life, looking happy and confident, is what gave Tiffany courage. *Maybe I won't feel miserable without makeup, after all*, she thought to herself. Over the next three months, Tiffany eventually stopped covering her skin completely. She felt lighter, freer. No more worrying about makeup rubbing off when she hugged someone or wondering if friends would treat her differently once they saw her real skin.

"You have to accept yourself," Tiffany said. "That is the first step to being at peace. This is your body, and you didn't do anything to cause this. You should not hide what makes you unique."

More Than a Model

Tiffany's story is just one example of how Winnie inspires people to see themselves differently. But she doesn't stop at leading by example. Winnie also uses her voice to challenge the way society talks about beauty, confidence, and identity.

In 2023, Winnie joined an extraordinary panel hosted by former First Lady Michelle Obama, alongside music stars H.E.R. and Kelly Rowland, as well as businessperson Tina Knowles-Lawson. The **cross-generational** group spoke about everything from trusting your instincts to breaking stereotypes.

During the discussion, Winnie revealed her least favourite interview question: "How are you so confident?" She then challenged the audience to think about what that question really means. "For being myself? For living in my own skin, I'm brave? Are you telling me I shouldn't be?"

As we already know, there's so much more to Winnie than her skin condition, which brings us to one of her proudest achievements ...

> ***"For being myself? For living in my own skin, I'm brave? Are you telling me I shouldn't be?"***

Winnie's exuberance and positivity are reflected in her supportive interactions with her fans.

"Being a Global Citizen is about having a vision for a better world and contributing to your community to work towards that vision," Winnie said at winning the Global Citizen Award.

CHAPTER 10
A Queen Is Crowned

In 2023, Winnie got one of the biggest honours of her career: the United Nations Global Citizen Award. This award celebrates Canadians who use their fame to make the world better.

The ceremony was in Toronto, and Winnie made it extra special by bringing along her mother and grandmother. Winnie wore a leopard print dress because the pattern is her grandmother's favourite. "I'm an embodiment of her," Winnie said proudly. "I live and breathe the fabulousness that is my grandmother."

Winnie posed for photos with her mom and grandmother—three generations holding the award together. The United Nations praised Winnie for "shattering **norms**" in fashion and speaking out for diversity and female empowerment. For Winnie, the award wasn't just a trophy. It was a reminder of why she does what she does.

"Being a Global Citizen is about having a vision for a better world and contributing to your community to work towards that vision," she said. "It's such a blessing to be recognized by your hometown community."

From runways to the United Nations, Winnie has never been just a model. She's also a role model. She's come a long way from that little Toronto girl who sat by the window, staring up at the stars, wishing she could change her skin. Today, she's building her own beauty empire, speaking on the world stage, and proving that real beauty is about rewriting the rules and lifting others up.

Her life is proof that being yourself is the ultimate power move.

Winnie's Wisdom

Winnie Harlow has faced challenges, made history, and stayed true to herself. Here are some truth bombs she's dropped over the years:

The Secret Sauce

"I just try to live my life every day with a few main things: honesty, respect, and love. Those things are very important to me and help me grow."

Fairness for All

"Equality rules! Regardless of what race, what colour, what sex, what nationality, what sexual orientation — regardless of who you are, equality should always rule!"

Glow Your Own Way

"Know for yourself what beauty is rather than looking to a magazine or even me for what beauty is."

Different = Awesome

"Know that feeling different is not wrong or negative. We are all different!"

Flip the Script

"The reason why I feel there is beauty in everything is because when I was young, I was picked on for something that today I feel is amazing."

Your Vibe, Your Life

"I think that people worry too much about what other people think, but what other people think isn't what's going to make you happy in your life, and it's your life to live."

Talk It Out

"My greatest lesson is something that I already knew: The people who are closest to you are the most important, and communication with them is so vital to life."

Don't Wait for an Invite

"When you don't see yourself, make yourself seen."

Don't Give Up

"Persevere. You have to always keep going. You're not going to get every job or be cast for every show, but you have to keep it moving and look ahead. It's hard. But it's essential."

The Same but Not

"We're all the same because we're all different. People always ask me, 'Would you like to say something to girls with vitiligo?' It's bigger than that. It's those girls with vitiligo, it's that little girl who didn't like her hair, it's that little girl who had freckles, it's that little boy who got teased because his lips were too big. It's everything."

Forget the Haters

"For every negative comment, there are a lot of positive ones as well. You can't let the words of nasty people get to you. It's not worth the energy."

Hustle Hard

"I wanted to take care of my mom and my sister and make my dad proud."

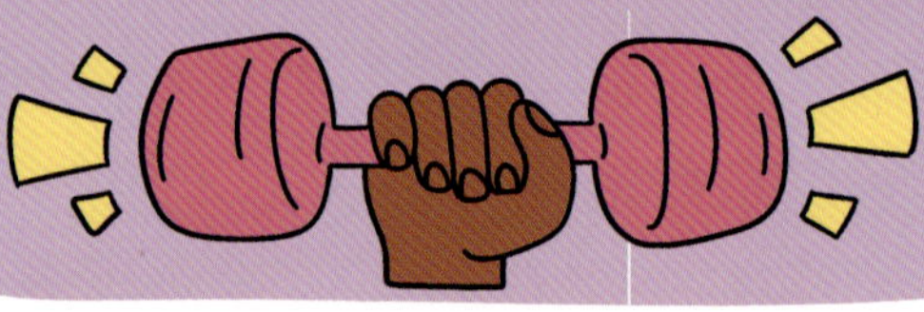

Confident Doesn't Mean Perfect

"Confidence doesn't eliminate **insecurities**, and insecurities don't mean you're not confident."

Lesson Learned

"My skin has been one of my greatest gifts. It has taught me, from the time I was a little girl, to use it as a megaphone: to be louder, prouder, and always fuelled by passion and love. It's helped me look beyond my own cover — and everyone else's too."

GLOSSARY

campaign: series of planned activities with a goal (e.g., an advertising campaign)

counselling: help from a professional to guide or give advice about an issue

cross-generational: involving people from different age groups

foundation: basis

inclusive language: the use of respectful words that value everyone regardless of gender, age, etc.

industry: business (e.g., the modelling industry)

insecurities: feelings of not being confident or sure of yourself

norms: unwritten rules or standards of behaviour

represented: shown or described in the media (news, ads, photos, TV, or online stories)

symmetrical: two matching halves; balanced

FURTHER READING

If You Want to Find Your Voice ...

Break the Mould: How to Find Your Place in the World, by Sinéad Burke

You Are A Champion, by Marcus Rashford

If You Want to Learn More About Vitiligo ...

How to Disappear Completely, by Ali Standish

If You Want To Read About How Others Handle Being "Different"...

Starfish, by Lisa Fipps

Normal: One Kid's Extraordinary Journey, by Magdalena Newman, Nathaniel Newman

Amy Land has been working with books since she got her first job at a Toronto library at age 15. She has created award-winning classroom books for Scholastic, Oxford, Rubicon, and Pearson, and always tries hard to make her writing fun and meaningful for young readers.

Amy felt a special connection to Winnie Harlow's story because her sister, Kate, is an artist with facial differences. Growing up close to someone who stands out has shaped the way Amy sees beauty and strength.

IMAGE CREDITS

Cover: Winnie Harlow attends the 'Loveless' premiere during the 70th Cannes Film Festival—©Andrea Raffin/Shutterstock; Endpaper: Winnie Harlow attends the 'Loveless' premiere during the 70th Cannes Film Festival—©Andrea Raffin/Shutterstock; 7: Michael Jackson at the 1997 Cannes Film Festival—©Featureflash Photo Agency/Shutterstock; 7: Jon Hamm at the 29th Annual Critics Choice Awards—©Kathy Hutchins/Shutterstock; 20: Tyra Banks at the "America's Got Talent" Live Show Red Carpet—©Kathy Hutchins/Shutterstock; 23: Winnie Harlow walks the runway at Desigual show during Mercedes-Benz Fashion Week—©Ovidiu Hrubaru/Shutterstock; 29: Winnie Harlow attends 2016 VH1 Hip Hop Honors: All Hail The Queens—©lev radin/Shutterstock; 32: Winnie Harlow walks in the 2018 Victoria's Secret runway show—©Bang Media International/Alamy; 36: Kyle Kuzma at the Monster Energy $50K Charity Challenge Celebrity Basketball Game —©Kathy Hutchins/Shutterstock; 36: Winnie Harlow at the WE Day California 2019—©Tinseltown/Shutterstock; 38: Winnie Harlow and Kyle Kuzma attend the amfAR Gala—©ZUMA Press, Inc./Alamy; 49: Jordan Chiles of the UCLA Bruins hugs Winnie Harlow after a college gymnastics meet between the Utah Utes and the UCLA Bruins at UCLA Pauley Pavilion—©Michael Yanow/NurPhoto/Shutterstock; 50: 2023 United Nations Association in Canada Global Citizen Award Gala Honoring Winnie Harlow—© George Pimentel/Shutterstock; 55: A model walks runway for Desigual Fall 2015 Runway show—©Sam Aronov/Shutterstock

chalk doodles—©KatePilko/Shutterstock; star pattern—©DPTYPE/Shutterstock; speech bubble pattern—©Anastasiia Hevko/Shutterstock; set of contemporary patterns—©oxygen_8/Shutterstock; colourful speech bubbles—©Alina Pear/Shutterstock; note bubbles—©Ramcreative/Shutterstock; set of quote boxes—©Polina Tomtosova/Shutterstock; notepad paper—©Your Local Llamacorn/Shutterstock; stack of books—©Alena Divina/Shutterstock; people standing in queue—©NotionPic/Shutterstock; woman refusing—©StockSmartStart/Shutterstock; megaphone—©Stranger Man/Shutterstock; hands holding smartphones—©maybealice/Shutterstock; ring—©BRO.vector/Shutterstock; travel luggage—©Paper Trident/Shutterstock; microphone—©Tartila/Shutterstock;

Library and Archives Canada Cataloguing in Publication

Title: Winnie Harlow : supermodel, entrepreneur, activist / Amy Land.
Names: Land, Amy (Author of Winnie Harlow), author.
Description: Series statement: Northern lights ; 1
Identifiers: Canadiana 20260184101 | ISBN 9781997872061 (hardcover)
Subjects: LCSH: Harlow, Winnie—Juvenile literature. | LCSH: Models (Persons)—Canada—Biography—Juvenile literature. | LCSH: Vitiligo—Patients—Canada—Biography—Juvenile literature. | LCSH: Businesswomen—Canada—Biography—Juvenile literature. | LCSH: Businesspeople—Canada—Biography—Juvenile literature. | LCGFT: Biographies.
Classification: LCC HD6073.M772 C35 2026 | DDC j746.9/2092—dc23

Publisher Cataloguing-in-Publication Data (U.S.)

Names: Land, Amy (Author of Winnie Harlow), author.
Title: Winnie Harlow : supermodel, entrepreneur, activist / Amy Land.
Description: First edition. | Oakville, Ontario : Plumleaf Press, 2026. | Series: Northern lights. | Includes bibliographical references. | Summary: "Winnie Harlow, who suffered from the rare skin condition known as vitiligo, defied her bullies by becoming a world-famous model and the founder of her own skincare brand"--Provided by publisher.
Identifiers: ISBN 978-1-99787-206-1 (hardcover)
Subjects: LCSH: Harlow, Winnie—Juvenile literature. | Models (Persons)—Canada—Biography—Juvenile literature. | Vitiligo—Patients—Canada—Biography—Juvenile literature. | Businesswomen—Canada—Biography—Juvenile literature. | BISAC: JUVENILE NONFICTION / Biography & Autobiography / Women. | JUVENILE NONFICTION / Biography & Autobiography / Performing Arts. | JUVENILE NONFICTION / Social Topics / Self-Esteem & Self-Reliance. | JUVENILE NONFICTION / Social Topics / Bullying. Classification: LCC HD9970.5.L36 2026 | DDC 338.7/66855092 B - dc23

Published in Canada by Plumleaf Press Inc. This is a first edition.

26 27 28 29 30 6 5 4 3 2 1

Cover design: Aubryn Harvey
Cover and Interior design: Aubryn Harvey, Rebecca Bender
Illustrations (pages: 4, 9, 11, 18, 45): Rebecca Bender

Plumleaf Press Inc.
100 Bronte Road, Unit 9, Oakville, ON, L6L 6L5
www.plumleafpress.com
Printed in China

MORE NORTHERN LIGHTS TITLES

Coming in 2027

Shai Gilgeous-Alexander

NBA MVP • Style Icon • Philanthropist

Autumn Peltier

Water-Rights Advocate • Indigenous Rights Activist

"True beauty lies in embracing your true self."

—*Winnie Harlow*